W9-BOL-745

SHARKS SET I

NURSE SHARKS

Heidi Mathea

ABDO Publishing Company

visit us at
www.abdopublishing.com

Published by ABDO Publishing Company, 8000 West 78th Street, Edina, Minnesota 55439. Copyright © 2011 by Abdo Consulting Group, Inc. International copyrights reserved in all countries. No part of this book may be reproduced in any form without written permission from the publisher. The Checkerboard Library™ is a trademark and logo of ABDO Publishing Company.

Printed in the United States of America, North Mankato, Minnesota.
042010
092010

 PRINTED ON RECYCLED PAPER

Cover Photo: Photolibrary
Interior Photos: © Bob Cranston/SeaPics.com p. 17; © D.R. Schrichte/SeaPics.com p. 8;
     © Jeff Jaskolski/SeaPics.com p. 15; Joe Marino p. 13;
     © Mark Strickland/SeaPics.com pp. 5, 18–19; © Masa Ushioda/SeaPics.com p. 11;
     Peter Arnold p. 21; Uko Gorter pp. 6–7, 9

Editor: BreAnn Rumsch
Art Direction & Cover Design: Neil Klinepier

Library of Congress Cataloging-in-Publication Data

Mathea, Heidi, 1979-.
 Nurse sharks / Heidi Mathea.
     p. cm. -- (Sharks)
 Includes index.
 ISBN 978-1-61613-427-3
 1. Nurse shark--Juvenile literature. I. Title.
 QL638.95.G55M38 2011
 597.3--dc22
                                    2010005541

CONTENTS

Nurse Sharks and Family

You might think nurse sharks care for others. This is not true. In fact, these sharks are quite lazy. They spend their days resting on the ocean's bottom.

Nurse sharks sometimes rest in groups of up to 40 individuals. Often, they pile on top of each other. Don't let these sleepy sharks fool you. At night, nurse sharks become fierce hunters!

There are three nurse shark species. These are the Short-tail Nurse Shark, the Nurse Shark, and the Tawny Nurse Shark.

Little is known about the secretive Short-tail Nurse Shark. Scientists are working hard to study and gain more information about these creatures.

Nurse sharks belong to the family Ginglymostoma.

WHAT THEY LOOK LIKE

Nurse sharks have thick bodies and wide heads. Their skin is covered in toothlike scales called denticles. These scales provide protection for the skin. Nurse sharks also have skeletons made of **cartilage**.

The Short-tail Nurse Shark is the smallest nurse shark species. It grows to just 30 inches (75 cm) long. This shark is dark brown.

On average, the Nurse Shark is 7 to 9 feet (2.1 to 2.7 m) long. It can grow up

GILL SLITS

PECTORAL FIN

6

to 14 feet (4.3 m). The Nurse Shark's tail, or caudal fin, can make up one-fourth its total length! Most adult Nurse Sharks weigh between 160 and 270 pounds (70 and 120 kg). They range from light yellowish tan to dark brown.

The largest Tawny Nurse Shark reported was 10.5 feet (3.2 m) long. These sharks are gray brown or brown in color.

SHORT-TAIL NURSE SHARK

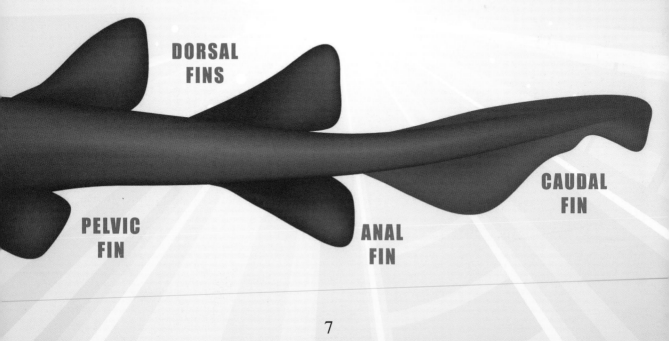

DORSAL
FINS

CAUDAL
FIN

PELVIC
FIN

ANAL
FIN

WHERE THEY LIVE

Nurse sharks prefer warm water. They occupy **tropical** and **subtropical** oceans. The Short-tail Nurse Shark lives in the western Indian Ocean. This shark spends its time on **insular** shelves and **continental shelves**.

Nurse Sharks are active at night.

Nurse Sharks live close to shore in the Atlantic and eastern Pacific oceans. During the day, they rest along reefs and rocky areas. The water there is 10 to 250 feet (3 to 75 m)

Where Do Nurse Sharks Live?

| Nurse Sharks | Tawny Nurse Sharks | Short-tail Nurse Sharks |

deep. These sharks move to shallower water at night to hunt.

Tawny Nurse Sharks swim in the Indian and western Pacific oceans. There, they live in coral reefs and lagoons. These sleepy sharks even occupy sandy surf areas. They are most common in water that is 16 to 98 feet (5 to 30 m) deep.

FOOD

Nurse Sharks are not fast swimmers. So, they prey on resting creatures. These **nocturnal** sharks love eating fish, especially stingrays. They also feed on **crustaceans**. Other tasty snacks include mollusks such as octopuses, squids, and clams.

Tawny Nurse Sharks eat a variety of creatures. These include sea urchins and crustaceans. They also feed on small fish such as surgeonfish, queenfish, and rabbitfish. Sometimes they even eat sea snakes. Short-tail Nurse Sharks feed on mollusks.

When hunting, nurse sharks swim slowly over the ocean floor. If they detect hidden prey, they suck it right out of its hiding hole!

Nurse Sharks suck prey into their mouths. So, they don't rely on their teeth for eating.

SENSES

Sharks have the same five senses you do. These are sight, taste, smell, touch, and hearing. Additional senses help them locate prey and mates.

Sharks have a sensitive lateral line system. This consists of sense **organs** along a shark's body. These organs allow sharks to detect vibrations in the water. This helps them find prey.

Using special sense organs in their heads, sharks can detect electric fields. All living animals give off their own electric field. This sense is another way nurse sharks find their next meals.

Nurse sharks have two barbels in front of the mouth. The sharks use them to find food by tasting and touching objects around them.

BABIES

Newborn nurse sharks are called pups. They hatch from eggs inside the mother and are born live. At birth, nurse shark pups have teeth. They also have dark spots on the skin. These spots fade as the sharks age. The pups are able to swim and hunt right away.

A female Nurse Shark is **pregnant** for about six months. She gives birth in a special nursery area. Often, these areas are close to shore. They provide newborn sharks access to food. A Nurse Shark can have up to 30 pups at a time. The pups are about 12 inches (30 cm) long at birth.

Tawny Nurse Shark mothers have up to 8 pups. When they are born, the pups are about 15 to 24 inches (38 to 61 cm) long.

The Tawny Nurse Shark is the more active swimming species.

ATTACK AND DEFENSE

Nurse sharks have small mouths and simple teeth. The teeth are made for crushing and gripping rather than for cutting. But, nurse sharks have powerful jaws and a strong bite. This makes them fearsome predators.

In addition, nurse sharks hunt at night. This allows them to catch prey that is resting that might normally be too speedy for these sleepy sharks.

A large Nurse Shark has almost nothing to fear except man. No predators regularly hunt these sharks.

Occasionally, a nurse shark becomes a larger shark's meal. These larger sharks include lemon, tiger, bull, and hammerhead sharks. Nurse sharks defend themselves by blending into the ocean's bottom.

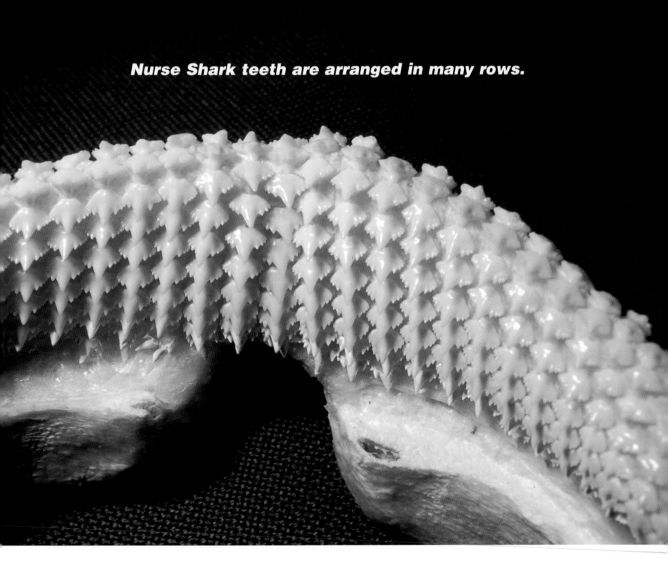

Nurse Shark teeth are arranged in many rows.

ATTACKS ON HUMANS

People like to swim and play in warm, shallow ocean waters. Nurse sharks also like these waters. So, contact between humans and nurse sharks happens often and continues to increase.

Generally, nurse sharks are dangerous only when bothered. They will often swim away when approached. However, they will bite to defend themselves. Their bites can cause serious harm.

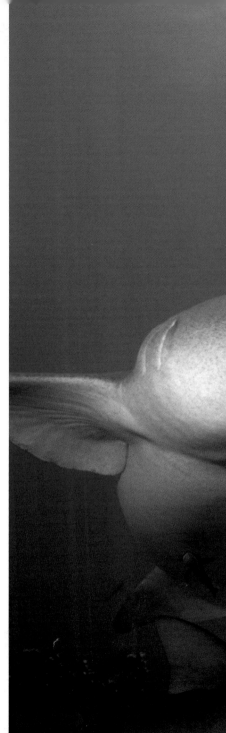

Like all sharks, nurse sharks should be treated with respect. This way, people and sharks can safely enjoy the world's oceans.

Tawny Nurse Shark and diver

NURSE SHARK FACTS

Scientific Name:

Nurse Shark	*Ginglymostoma cirratum*
Tawny Nurse Shark	*Nebrius ferrugineus*
Short-tail Nurse Shark	*Pseudoginglymostoma brevicaudatum*

Average Size:

Nurse sharks grow 30 inches (75 cm) to 14 feet (4.3 m) in length.

Where They're Found:

Nurse sharks live in coastal waters in tropical and subtropical seas.

GLOSSARY

cartilage (KAHR-tuh-lihj) - the soft, bendable connective tissue in the skeleton. A person's nose and ears are made of cartilage.

continental shelf - a shallow, underwater plain forming a continent's border. It ends with a steep slope to the deep ocean floor.

crustacean (kruhs-TAY-shuhn) - any of a group of animals with a hard shell and jointed legs. Crabs, lobsters, and shrimps are all crustaceans.

insular - of or having to do with an island.

nocturnal - active at night.

organ - a part of an animal or a plant composed of several kinds of tissues. An organ performs a specific function. The heart, liver, gallbladder, and intestines are organs of an animal.

pregnant - having one or more babies growing within the body.

subtropical - relating to an area where average temperatures range between 55 and 68 degrees Fahrenheit (13 and 20°C).

tropical - relating to an area with an average temperature above 77 degrees Fahrenheit (25°C) where no freezing occurs.

WEB SITES

To learn more about nurse sharks, visit ABDO Publishing Company on the World Wide Web at **www.abdopublishing.com**. Web sites about nurse sharks are featured on our Book Links page. These links are routinely monitored and updated to provide the most current information available.

INDEX

A

Atlantic Ocean 8
attacks 18

B

body 6, 12

C

cartilage 6
color 6, 7, 14

D

defense 6, 16, 18
denticles 6

E

eggs 14
environment 4, 8,
    9, 10, 14, 16, 18

F

food 10, 12, 14, 16

G

groups 4

H

head 6, 12
hunting 4, 9, 10,
    12, 14, 16

I

Indian Ocean 8, 9

J

jaws 16

L

lateral line 12

M

mouth 16

P

Pacific Ocean 8, 9
predators 16
pups 14

R

reproduction 12, 14

S

senses 12
size 6, 7, 14
skin 6, 14

T

tail 7
teeth 14, 16